CAROL-ANN MOFFITT-NEICH

Copyright © 2024 by Carol-Ann Moffitt-Neich

Paperback: 978-1-964744-61-2
eBook: 978-1-964744-62-9
Library of Congress Control Number: 2024914579

All rights reserved. No part of this publication may be reproduced, distributed, or transmitted in any form or by any electronic or mechanical means, without the prior written permission of the publisher, except in the case of brief quotations embodied in critical reviews and certain other noncommercial uses permitted by copyright law.

This Book is a work of fiction. Names, characters, places, and incidents either are the product of the author's imagination or are used fictitiously. Any resemblance to actual persons, living or dead, events, or locales is entirely coincidental.

Ordering Information:

Prime Seven Media
518 Landmann St.
Tomah City, WI 54660

Printed in the United States of America

You colour the world
With your art
You colour the world
With your talent
You colour the world
With your beauty
You colour the world
In glowing rainbows
You colour the world
From top to bottom
You colour the world
In ink
Keep colouring the world
For the world needs more colour

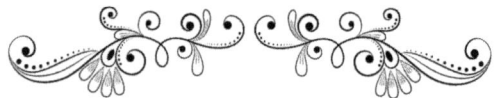

Take the time to heal
It doesn't matter how long it takes
It doesn't matter what it looks like
You are worth the wait
You are worth every way it looks
You are worth everything
Never forget your worth

GUJARATI-ENGLISH VOCABULARY

Gujarati	Transliteration	Meaning	Unit
સુથાર (m.)	suthār	carpenter	5
સુધી	sudhī	until (time or place)	2
સુંદર	sumdar	beautiful	3
સુઇ જવું	sūī javum	to go to bed	5
સૂતર (n.)	sūtar	thread, cotton	15
સૂર્યાસ્ત (m.)	sūryāst	sunset	14
સૂર્યોદય (m.)	sūryoday	sunrise	14
સૂંઘવું (t.)	sūmghvum	smell	9
સેકંડ (f.)	sekamd	second	7
સેક્રેટરી (f./m.)	sekretarī	secretary	6
સેંકડો (m.)	semkdo	hundred, century, hundreds (adj.)	15
સેંડલ (.)	semdal	sandal (not. dict.)	15
સો (m.)	so	hundred	7
સોનેરી	sonerī	golden	14
સોમવાર (m.)	somvār	Monday	7
સોસાયટી (f.)	sosāyaṭī	society, housing association	6
સૌ	sau	all	6
સ્ત્રી (f.)	strī	woman	1
સ્થિતિ (f.)	sthiti	state, condition, status	13
સ્નાન (n.)	snān	bath	5
સ્નાન કરવું	snān karvum	to take a bath, bathe	5
સ્નેહી	snehī	Dear... (Unit 8.5)	8
સ્પષ્ટ	spaṣṭ	clear, evident, plain	11
સ્મરણ (n. pl.)	smaraṇ	Yours... (Unit 8.5)	8
સ્વભાવ (m.)	svabhāv	charactger, nature	8
સ્વરાજ (n.)	svarāj	self-government	15
સ્વર્ગવાસી	svargvāsī	living in heaven, deceased, late	8
સ્વીકારવું (t.)	svīkārvum	accept, receive	14
હકીકત (f.)	hakīkat	fact, news, detailed account	6
હજાર (m.)	hajār	thousand	7
હજી (પણ)	hajī (paṇ)	still, yet, even now	6
હજી સુધી	hajīsudhī	still, yet, up till now	7
હતું	hatum	was	2
હમાલ (m.)	hamāl	coolie, porter	9

ગુજરાતી	લિપ્યંતર	અર્થ	પાઠ
હમેશાં	**hameśāṃ**	*always*	4
હવા (f.)	**havā**	*wind, breeze*	14
હવા ખાવી	**havā khāvī**	*get some fresh air*	14
હવે	**have**	*now*	2
હસ્તમેળાપ (m.)	**hastmeḷāp**	*joining hands, N. of part of wedding*	8
હળવું (i.)	**haḷvuṃ**	*be familiar, friendly*	12
હળવુંમળવું (t.)	**haḷvuṃmaḷvuṃ**	*mix, meet*	12
હા	**hā**	*yes*	1
હા જી	**hā jī**	*yes (formal)*	1
હાડકું (n.)	**hāḍkuṃ**	*bone*	11
હાથ (m.)	**hāth**	*hand, arm*	4
હાથ જોડવા	**hāth joḍvā**	*join hands in greeting, supplication*	14
હાફપેંટ	**hāphpeṃṭ**	*shorts*	12
હાલચાલ (f.)	**hālcāl**	*movement, manners*	13
હાસવું	**hāsvuṃ**	*to laugh*	9
હાસ્ય (n.)	**hāsya**	*laugh, laughing*	15
હિસાબ (m.)	**hisāb**	*calculation, account*	6
હિંદુ (m.f./adj.)	**hindu**	*Hindu*	1
હિંસા (f.)	**hiṃsā**	*violence*	9
હીંચકો (m.)	**hīṃcko**	*swing*	14
હું	**huṃ**	*I*	1
હોટલ/હોટેલ (f.)	**hoṭal/hoṭel**	*hotel, cafe*	5
હોવું	**hovuṃ**	*to be*	5
હોશિયાર	**hośiyār**	*clever*	1

You lay yourself bare to the world
For all to see
For all to comment
For all to judge
You show what an amazing person you are
You show how to be real
You show how to care
You show how to do what's right
Even when you are bullied
Believe me when I say
You are appreciated
You are showing the world
How to stand up and do what's right

Do you know how lucky you are
You are lucky that you woke up this morning
You are lucky that you have clothes to wear
You are lucky that you have food to eat
You are lucky you have a bed to sleep in
You are lucky that you can see this
Appreciate
How lucky you are

Remember they only hate you
Because they cannot be you
They only hate you
Because they are jealous of you
They only hate you
Because they see you living your best life
They only hate you
Because they are only looking in from the outside
They only hate you
Because they see they could not bring you down
No they do not hate you
They hate themselves

You are a diamond
Everything you have been through
Have made you what you are today
For you have been through so much
You have been through so much pressure
You can not make diamonds without pressure
You have been made into a diamond

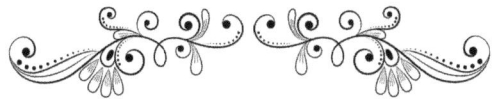

You are evolving into the person
You have always meant to be
Embrace the change
Embrace the new you
Embrace the person you were always meant to be
For this new you
Is amazing and powerful
Never forget how amazing you are
Never forget how powerful you are
Embrace you with loving arms
Embrace you with a loving heart
Embrace the new you

You are filled with magic
The magic to change your world
The magic to change your life
You are filled with magic
Magic is all around you
Just look around and see it everywhere
For life is truly magical
Your life is magical

When is the last time
You were told
You are special
You are perfect
Just the way you are
You should be proud
of yourself
Just as I'm proud of you
When was the last time
Some one told you
How proud they were of you
It's been a while
Let me tell you today
You are special
You are perfect
I'm proud of you
Today and everyday

Everyday we change
We change and evolve everyday
Change for the better
Learn and grow
Learn from the everyday
Grow from the everyday
Make the changes you want to see
For everyday we change

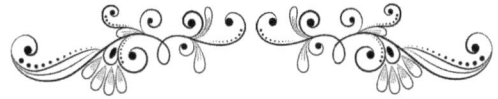

You walk with a smile
You walk proud
They will never know
Just how much
You are hurting
Just how much
You have been through
Because your smile is bright
Because you know it will get better
Because you know you can get through this
Because you are brave and a fighter
Keep walking with that smile
Keep walking with your head held high
Keep being the fighter you are
Keep fighting for that life you deserve

You have the power
The power to do what you dream
The power to be who you want
The power to go where you desire
The power to live your best life
You are powerful
Never forget
How powerful you are

Let go of your past
Make way for your new beginning
For the past is over
You can't change it
It is what it is
It was what it was
It helped make you who you are today
Be proud of the person you are
Be proud of everything you got through
Be proud of everything you have achieved
So let go of what you can not change
Make room for the life that is on the way
For there is a new chapter about to begin

I'm proud of you
You are amazing
You are special
You are unique
Never forget
Who you are
Never forget
I'm proud of you

Don't worry about tomorrow
For tomorrow hasn't happened
Don't worry about the what if's
Don't worry about the maybe's
Don't waste your time on the unknown
For tomorrow is another life
Look at today
Enjoy today
Take the energy worrying about tomorrow
Put that energy into enjoying today
Enjoy the here and now

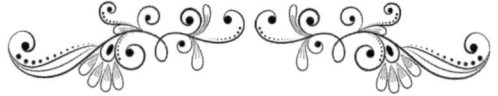

Never forget to be proud of yourself
I am proud of everything you have achieved
I am proud of everything you are doing
I am proud of everything you are going to do
Be proud of you too

ON THE WINGS OF EMPOWERMENT

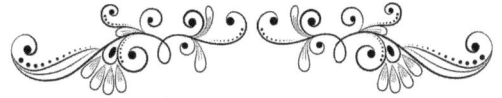

If you can dreamed it
you can do it
You have to believe it
You have to believe
you can achieve it
You have to have faith
in yourself
You have to have faith
in your destiny
You have to have faith
in your dreams
So dream it
Dream big
Believe it
Do it

You are perfect just the way you are
Don't try and be someone else
They don't have what you have
You are special
They see how special you are
They just may be trying to be you

ON THE WINGS OF EMPOWERMENT

Clear your mind
Clear your thoughts
Think about you
Think about what you want
Think about what you need
Think about how to get it
Think about how to achieve it
Think about your future
Think about your future happiness
Think about you for a change
Put you first

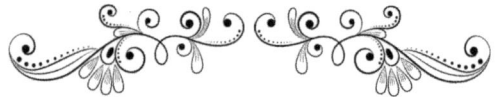

Fight for your dreams
Fight for what you want
Never give up fighting
For your dreams are worth fighting for
Fight until your dreams come true

You are here for a reason
You are here for a purpose
Never think you are not needed
Never think you are not worthy
Never think you are not relevant
Never think you are not enough
You are special in every way
You are amazing just as you are
You were made to be remarkable
You are incredible
Never forget
Who you are

Don't accept anything less than what you need
Don't accept anything less then what you deserve
Don't accept anything less than what you want
You know your worth
Even if many don't know it
You know it, that's what matters
So don't accept anything less than your worth

As one door closes
Don't be afraid
Look ahead
For the doors awaiting you
Are hiding adventures
You could only imagine
Take a leap of faith
Open one
See where your tomorrow
Leads you
See where the future
Awaits to be discovered

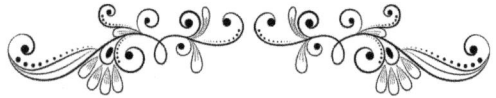

Don't give up
Keep going
Keep dreaming
Keep being you

Take a look at yourself
A really good look
You have worked hard
You have overcome it all
You have made it look easy
You have achieved what you wanted
You have achieved what nobody thought you could
You are strong and determined
to do it all achieve it all
You can do it, and so much more
than you think you can
Go out there and keep being the
amazing brilliant determined you

Everything worth having
Takes time
Takes effort
Takes patience
It will be worth it
Worth the wait
Worth the toil
Worth the assiduity
It will be worth it

Life wasn't meant to be easy
Life wasn't meant to pass you by
If it was easy you wouldn't have
any thing to dream of
You wouldn't have anything to strive for
You wouldn't have anything to achieve
You wouldn't have anything to work for
What would get you out of bed in the morning
What would you wish for
What would you dream about
So get up and start living
Get up and start dreaming
Get up and start doing it all
Life wasn't meant to pass you by

Don't give up
Don't give up on you
Keep going
You are going to make it
You are going to succeed
Just don't give up

If you fail
That means you have tried
If you fall
That means you have tried
If you stumble
That means you have tried
Success never comes to those
Who don't try
Success never comes to those
Who don't dream
Success never comes to those
Who don't give their all
Go out there
Try, dream, give it your all

You are incredible
You exude beauty
Without even trying
Without even knowing
Just how amazing you are

If you stumble
If you fall
Get back up
Smile
Keep going
You are not alone
Who hasn't stumbled
Who hasn't fallen
It's how you get back up
That matters
It's how you keep going
That matters

Never forget just how special you are
Never forget what you have achieved
Never forget what you have been through
Never forget how strong you are
Never forget how resilient you are
Never forget you can do anything
you set your mind to
Never forget you have the ability to
make your dreams come true
Never forget you are a warrior

Looking back is good
To see how far you have come
How much you have achieved
How much you have grown
How much you have changed
How you now perceive yourself
How many things you now wont do
How much you now value yourself
How many boundaries you now have
How much you now know you are worth
But the trick is to know how to look forward

There is no failure in life
It's not a failure you haven't met your goals
You are working towards them
You will just keep going
Just keep working towards them
For you shall meet your gaols
It will just take time
Just take longer
But you will get there
Just don't give up

Looking ahead
What do you feel
What does it evoke
What do you wish for
What makes you smile
What makes you stop and dream
What does your future look like
What makes the days worth living
Stop and think about what's ahead
Stop and think about what makes you happy
Stop and take the time to dream
Stop and start to live the life you want

If your crown slips
Just straighten it back up
Always remember you are a queen
Queens always wear their crowns with pride
Step out and prove to them you
were meant to be a queen
You were meant to wear that crown
So straighten that crown and smile
Keep walking tall
Never forget you are a queen

Be the light in your day
Be the light in someones else's day
Shine your light
Bright for everyone to see
Show them you are shinning
Show them just how bright your light is
Show them just how bright you are
Shine that light for the world to see
For you are a shinning light
In everyones day
Glowing strong
Glowing bright

I'm working on my biggest masterpiece
My biggest masterpiece of all time
I'm going to be so proud
I hope you will be proud too
For this masterpiece is precious
I hope it's precious to you
For I am my biggest masterpiece
I am proud of what I have achieved
I hope you are proud of me too

Why would you do
Something you want
Something you dream about
Something you wish
But not put in every effort
To make it come true
To fulfill your dreams
Do everything you can
Do it with every ounce of your being
With every breathe you take
To make it happen
To never regret trying
To never wonder
What if only

I wish you could see
What I see
I wish you could see
What every one sees
For what I see
For what everyone sees
Is the most beautiful person
Inside and out
I wish you could see
What I see

Pick up your phone
Now go and stand in front of your mirror
Go on
Go and do it
Now take a look at the reflection
looking back at you
Have a good look
Do you know what that person has been through
Do you know how much they have overcome
Do you know how much they have achieved
Do you know how proud I am of you
YOU ARE SPECIAL
YOU ARE UNIQUE
You have so much more to come
So many more amazing moments to experience
As of this moment your life has just begun
Every minute is a new minute of your life
A new minute for your dreams to come true
Now read this again
I am proud of you
You are special
You are unique

You are real
You are you
You are who you
Were meant to be
You are who you
Were meant to become
You wouldn't want
To be anyone else
For you are unique

The best is yet to come
Your current situation is not the end
It's not final
Tomorrow is your new current
And yet still not your final
Next week is your new current
And yet still not your final
Next month is your new current
And yet still not your final
Next year is your new current
And yet still not your final
There is no final
The best is yet to come

Give it your all
Give it everything you have
Give it the best you have to give
Never will you wonder
What if
If you have given it your all

You will never know
The true impact
You make on someones life
For you just being you
You being kind
You being an ear to listen
You being a shoulder to lean on
You being the bright light
In someones day
Has more impact than you
Will ever know

Don't stop now
You have come so far
You have done so much work
To stop now
Keep going
Don't stop until you reach your goal
For you have come too far
To stop now
Don't stop now
You can do it

Someone is out there today
Smiling
Because you have made a difference
In their lives
Someone is out there today
Alive
Because you have made an impact
In their lives
Someone is out there today
Achieving
Because you have had faith
In their ability
Someone is out there today
Living their best life
Because you believed in them
You did that

What was once lost
Was lost for a reason
It was not meant for you
There was something better for you
Just waiting for you to find it
Just waiting to change your life
Just waiting to change your world

You will never know the difference
You have in someones life
For you just being there for them
You may never hear it being said
But look around and see the impact
You have made on so many lives
Keep being the amazing person
You are
Never forget how needed you are
Never forget how important you are
Never forget what a difference
You make in this world

You are stronger than you know
You are wiser than you think
You bring happiness to more
than you could imagine
Believe in the power of you
Believe in the power of your life
For you are more valuable than you will ever know
Your presence means so much
To so many
Never stop being you

I sit here pondering life
Pondering my life
What has past
Then I realised
I can do anything I want
Anything
For the first time
I only have to please myself
So it's up to me to go out there
Live my best life
Anything I want
Anywhere I want to go
What an amazing thought
What an amazing opportunity
What an amazing life I've had
What an amazing life I am still to have

You are what you think
Make sure you are thinking
With positive thoughts
Think how blessed you are
Think how successful you are
Think how lucky you are
Think how abundant you are
Think only positive thoughts
As you are what you think

Never let that one person in your past
Be the definition of your future
They are in your past for a reason
They are not your future
Your future is not defined by them
Your future is not defined by their words
Your future is not defined by their actions
Your future is defined by you
Your future is defined by your actions
Your future is defined by your words
Your future is defined by your dreams
Remember that always

Your beauty is shinning through
For everyone to see
It shines from within
For they can't but see your beauty
Your truth is beautiful
Your honesty is beautiful
Your good heart is beautiful
You are beautiful inside and out
Never forget just how beautiful you are

Don't live in yesterday
Living in the "could of beens"
Don't worry about tomorrow
Living in the "what ifs"
Live in the "today"
The right now
Don't miss anything
Worrying about your past or future
Live in the moment
Enjoy every moment
Of every day

You deserve everything you have ever dreamed of
You deserve to live your best life
You deserve to be loved
You deserve a life full of joy
A life full of happiness
A life full of love
A life full of peace
A life full of contentment
You deserve it all

Do you know what some are thinking
when they look at you
They think you are the luckiest person on earth
You have family to love
Family who love you
Family and friends who support you
You are looking at others and longing
For what they portray their life to be
But do you know how many people
Are looking at your life and are dreaming
Just to have a fraction of what you have
To have the love and support you have
Never forget you are living someone eles's
Dream life

You're not your mistakes
Your mistakes do not define you
Mistakes are there to learn from
Mistakes are the past
Not your future
Not who you are
For who you are
Is who you are today
Who you are tomorrow

Watch how your enemies
Want to become your friends
Because you shine from within
You know your worth
You speak the truth
You show how to be real
You show how to step up
You show how to be a warrior
Just because you are you
They can't deny your energy
Because they now realise
There is no one like you

You can live your life
Like the darkness of night
Or you can live your life
In the colour of day
It's up to you
It's your choice
Make a conscience choice
Everyday

You know what you don't want in life
You know what you don't want in a relationship
But do you know what you do want
Take the time to see what you want
How to get it
How to achieve it
How you will feel once you have done it
How you will feel living the life
You do want
The only person stopping this
Is you

Every road I take
Leads me to a new destiny
Every path I take
Leads me to my new life
Every step I take
Leads me happiness
Don't be afraid to take that first step
To your happiness

Life can change in an instant
We make plans
Plans for tomorrow
Plans for next week
Plans for next year
But life can change in an instant
Make sure your plans
Can change with you
Don't let life pass you by
Because of those plans
The maybe's
Take each possibility
Each opportunity
To live the life of your dreams

You cannot change your birth circumstances
But you can change your outcome
You can change your attitude
You can change your expectations
You can change your surroundings
You can change your life
You can change your world

Walk with a smile
Watch everyone smile
As they walk by
Be kind
Watch everyone around
Be kind to one another
Show love
Watch everyone show love
Show love, show kindness and smile
Yes
You can change the world
One smile at a time

Never give up
Fighting for love
Fighting for happiness
Fighting for you
For you wouldn't give up
On others
So don't give up on you
You are worth fighting for

You've over come so much
In your life
You are not the same person
You once were
You have grown
You have evolved
Into an astonishing person
Stand tall
For you have fought
To become everything you are
Right now
Everything you once thought you couldn't achieve
Everything you could only dream of
Stand tall
Stand proud

The more you shine
Within
The more you'll shine
On the outside

Let go of what is not benefiting you
Let go of all that extra baggage
It's a heavy load you don't need
It's just weighing you down
Let it go
Feel the weight come of your shoulders
Let it go
Now go out there and live your life
The way you should be living
Free and light
Free to do anything you want

You are irreplaceable
Your presence is felt
But your absence screams
Never doubt your value

Look back on your life
See how everything happened
Just the way it was supposed to
Everything happened for a reason
Everyone in your life
Was there for a reason
Whether they were there for a short time
Whether they were there for a long period
Whether they are still there
They were there for a reason
Your life happened just as it was supposed to
Embrace your past
Embrace your future

Nothing good
Nothing exciting
Ever came from
Compliancy
Make sure
You are being true
To you

Let what's meant for you
Come to you
Don't think you are not worthy
Don't think it's not meant for you
It is
It's coming because you deserve it
You deserve every opportunity
To be happy
To live your best life
So embrace what's coming
With open arms

You can live your life
In black and white
You can live you life
In colour
Do you live
In the darkness of the past
Or
Do you live in the colour of the future

Having faith in yourself
Believing in yourself
Is what truly matters
Is what is going to make your dreams come true
Is what is going to let you never give up on yourself
What others think
What others believe about you
Is not for you to be concerned about
What truly matters is what you believe about yourelf
What you think about yourself
What you think you can achieve
That's the only person you need to worry about
YOU

Life is a series of adventures
Adventures in everyday
Adventures we have planned
Adventures of the unknown
One thing is sure
Life is a series of adventures

You are ready

You are worthy

Of everything

Coming for you

Of everything

You have dreamed

Of everything

You can imagine

You are deserving

Never forget

How astonishing you are

What you do next
Is what defines you
Not what has been
Not what went wrong
But how you take your next step
Is what defines you

I'm so very proud of you
I'm proud of the woman you have become
I'm proud of the mother you are
I'm proud of the future you are creating
For you and your family
I'm proud of the courage you have
To make the changes in your life
I'm proud of the resilience you have
To change your world
I'm proud of the way
You are showing your children
To never give up on your dreams
I'm proud how you are showing them
If you work hard enough
You can achieve anything
You set your mind to
But most of all
I'm just proud of you
Never forget how amazing you are

If you don't believe in you
Then nobody else will
Believe you can
Believe in you

Your fire within
Is just waiting for you
To ignite it
To use it
To burn through the past
To set fire to your future
For your future is brighter
With the fire that is within you
So ignite it
Let it burn bright
Let it burn hot
Just let it burn for you

You are a mystery
Let them wonder
Let them imagine
For being a mystery
Is unique
You keep being you
You keep being a mystery

Appreciate you
Appreciate everything you have been through
Appreciate everything you have achieved
Appreciate everything you have worked so hard for
Appreciate the struggles you came through
Appreciate the tears you dried
Appreciate the depths you climbed out of
Appreciate every win you had
Appreciate the moment of happiness
Appreciate every moment to joy
Appreciate every moment of love
For you are amazing
For you have fought and won
For you have worked so hard
To get where you are
So take the time
To appreciate you

Don't let anyone put you down
Don't let anyone bring you down to their level
Stay strong in who you are
Stay strong in your values
Stay strong in your beliefs
Stay strong in knowing your worth
Believe in who you are
Believe in you

Have you been told lately
How loved you are
How amazing you are
What a great job your doing
How you have brought joy to so many
That you bring a smile to the people you meet
How proud of you
I am
Have you been told lately
I hope so
I hope someone tells you everyday

Hold on to your dream
It's your dream
Don't let anyone talk you out of it
Don't let anyone take it away from you
Your dreams are yours
No one else's
Hold tight
Dream big

Put yourself first
It's not being selfish
It's not loving yourself to much
It's not being self centred
You need to put yourself first
Look after yourself
Look after your mind
Look after your body
Look after your heart
Look after your soul
For you can not look after anyones elses
Until you have looked after your first

Don't be afraid to be the first
Don't be afraid to be the last
Don't be afraid to do something new
Don't be afraid to do something old
Don't be afraid of life
Just don't be afraid to live

Trust in your story
For your story is just for you
You are the main character
Have faith in the pages
Have faith in the chapters
Have faith in the ending
Trust that the ending
Is exactly the way you have written it it your head
Trust that the story you have dreamt about
Is the one you are living
Enjoy every minute of your story
Let it unfold just the way it should
Have trust in your story

Just because things end
Doesn't mean they can't be the beginning
Of something wonderful
Take a look at the new direction
Before you give up
That ending just made way
For something you could only dream of

If you want it
Really want it
Fight for it
Fight everyday
For what you want
For that dream
You can do it
Don't give up
Keep going
Until you have it
Until you achieve it
So go out there and fight
Fight hard everyday
For what you want
Never give up

Making your wishes come true
Sometimes means giving up
On what you think you need
On what you think should be
On what you think is right
Step back
Let what is meant for you
Come to be
To make your wish come true

If you are not pursuing your dreams
Because you are afraid
Because you are scared
Of the unknown
You will never achieve them
Your dreams will never come true
You need to take a risk
You need to step out of your comfort zone
You need to take a leap of faith
Even if you fail
You will never have to wonder
About the what ifs
But what if you succeed
What if all your dreams come true
How amazing could your life be
If you only take that leap of faith

Stop thinking the worst
Stop thinking nothing will workout
Start hoping for the best
Start believing it will work out
Start thinking positively about life
Start believing in yourself
Start believing in your life

Don't wait until tomorrow to start
For then today is a day wasted
Today could of been the first day
Of the rest of your life
The first day
Of living your dreams
The first day
Of seeing the change you wanted
The first day
Of being the change you wanted
So don't wait another day
Don't wait until you are another day older
Start today
For today is here
For you to start living your dreams

Every day you get up
A little bit stronger
A little bit wiser
A little bit happier
The important thing is
You get up
Every day

If life is getting you down
If you are not happy
Imagine how unhappy you will be in the future
If you don't make the change needed
The change to go out there and live the life you want
Just imagine in a few years how
despondent you will be
Do you really want to be the person
walking around with regrets
I don't think so
So go and do something about it
Make today the day you made yourself happy
Make today the day you changed your life

Your beauty shines from within
Your beauty out shines the rest
You are not like anyone else
You are a beacon shining the way
You are showing how to let your inner beauty
Out shine your outer beauty
For that is a rare quality not many poses
Keep shinning bright
Day and night

Everything in life is a lesson
Everything that has happened to you
Everything that is happening to you
It's all a lesson
To be the person you are now
To be the amazing person you will be tomorrow
For everything that life has taught you
Has made you the person you are now
Has got you to where you are
There are many lessons in life
Don't ever stop welcoming these lessons
Don't ever stop feeling blessed

Stop waiting for the changes you think you need
Before you are going to be happy
Be happy now
The changes will come when you are happy
The changes will only make you happier
If you wait until the changes
You may be waiting a life time
They may never come
Be happy now

Look for the rainbow
After the storm in your life
For after any storm
A beautiful rainbow appears
Look for that elusive pot of gold
For there is always some gold to be found
After a great storm
You may not find it straight away
It may take some time to realise
Just what the gold is
Never stop looking
It's there
Just waiting to be found

Be strong enough to believe in yourself
Be strong enough to do what you say
Be strong enough to try again
Be strong enough to walk away if need be
Be strong enough to start again
But most of all
Believe in yourself

What is destined for you
Can not be hurried
What is destined for you
Can not be pushed aside
What is destined for you
Shall come when the time is right
What is destined for you
Shall put in perspective
The life you have chosen
The life you have lived
What is destined for you
No one can take away

Your life is unfolding
Just the way it should
Just the way you dreamed
You have worked so hard
For the life you now live
It is all working out for you
Just the way it should
You are worth it
You are worth the world

You respect their honesty
You respect their kindness
You respect their ability to follow through
Their never give up attitude
You respect their life ethics
Don't stand there and admire it
On someone else
Be it
Admire it on yourself
Have those values yourself
Respect those values on yourself
Be the person you stand there and admire

You are capable of more than you think
You are capable of enduring more than you know
You are stronger than you could ever imagine
Have the faith in yourself
Have the belief in yourself
That you can do it
You can do anything
You put your mind to

Your path in life is purely your own
No one else has the same path
No one else will journey down the road you take
For each of us are travelling down a different road
We are all on a different journey in life
So don't worry about anyone else's road
What their road looks like
You may think their road is smooth
But you don't know how far along
before it gets bumpy
So concentrate on your road
Concentrate on smoothing your journey ahead
For your journey is the only one that matters

Some things in life can't be changed
Some things shouldn't be changed
Instead of trying to change
Embrace your uniqueness
Embrace what makes you different
For these things are what make you stand out
These are what make you shine above the rest
So embrace you
For you are truly
Extraordinary

What you think
You become
Your thoughts
Are your reality
Believe in your dreams
Believe you can
And you will
Then do it
This is the reaction
To what you think
The reaction to your thoughts
So think big
Think like you
Already have it
Already live it

Don't hold on to the past
Let it go
So you can make way for what is to come
For what is to come
Is better than what you're holding on to
Better than the past
Is better than you can imagine

Let your mind
Lead you to your dreams
Let your mind
Lead you to your path
Let your mind
Lead you to your life's journey
For your mind
Is always looking for the best
Path and journey for you
Your mind is always on
Wishing, hoping, praying
Your dreams become your reality

We all have the capability to change our lives
The capability to changed our world
One day at a time
One wish at a time
One action at a time
Make today the day
You start to change
Your life
You start to change
Your world

When people meet you
They are confused
Because they had already
Formed an opinion about you
Then they meet you
You leave them
Wondering who you really are
For you are kind
Refined
Wise
Your facetes shine
When you speak people listen
For you have lived a life
That has taught you so many lessons
That you can relate to so many
You have empathy for any situation
Anyone you come across
Keep being the beautiful soul you are
Keep being the one who leaves them
Dismayed

Your rewards are on there way
You deserve everything coming for you
For you have worked so hard
To get where you are
You deserve happiness
You deserve love
You deserve joy
You deserve everything
That is coming your way

No matter how hard things seem
No matter how much you have gone through
No matter what life has thrown you
There is always something to be grateful for
Take a look at what has happened
For your hardest times
May have saved you from a world
Unimaginable
Look back and be grateful
That where you are now
Is somewhere you could never of imagined
In your darkest times
You have gotten through them
And are now smiling
There is always something to be
Grateful for

You have the power within
To make your dreams come true
To achieve everything you have ever wanted
That power is just waiting for you to use
Just waiting for you to believe in yourself
Just waiting for you to harness that power
And believe you can achieve it all
Using that amazing power within

One simple act of kindness
Can change a persons life
Can change their day
May even have the power
To change their life
They will never forget your kindness
That act will then have a ripple effect
For they will then be able to have the same effect
On someone else's life
Your simple act of kindness can
start to change the world

The universe knows what you want
The universe knows what you need
The universe is sending you a future
Full of abundance
Full of love and laughter
That you deserve
That you have been waiting for
Don't give up
It's on it's way

You sparkle
You shine
As you travel through life
Never lose your sparkle
Never lose your shine
For life sometimes rubs off
Some of your sparkle
So never lose yourself
In the everyday hardships of life
Never let anyone take away your sparkle
Always remember to shine
Then you will always sparkle

You know you deserve happiness
You know you deserve to be cherished
You know you deserve to be loved
You deserve everything life has to offer
The question is
Do you believe it
You know you deserve it
But you need to believe it

There's a fine line
You talking about that fine line
About being careful
You are already there
You have already crossed it
It's time to take back control
It's time to look what you need to do for you
It's time to put your future first
It's time to put you first
Move forward
Don't look back
Leave that line far in the distance

Be true to yourself
Be true of what lays within
For you are perfect just the way you are
Don't change to fit in
Don't change because you have doubts
Believe in yourself
Be true to yourself
You are perfect
Just as you are

Why are you looking back
Why are you living in the past
Why are you relapsing
You have come so far
You are here for a reason
You have overcome so much
You are an inspiration to so many
You need to start believing in you
You need to start seeing what others see
You need to be your own inspiration
You need to step into your next chapter
You need allow yourself to live again
You need to allow yourself to love again

Trust in you
Trust you are who you are meant to be
Trust you are perfect just as you are
Trust in the person you have become
Trust the person you have become
Is where you are supposed to be
Trust in yourself

Don't give up
Don't let doubt be the reason
You give up
Don't give up
You can do it
Have faith in yourself
Have faith in your dreams
Have faith it will work out
Have faith it will be everything you dreamed of
So don't give up
Believe in yourself
You can do it

Your life may have come tumbling down
But you get to rebuild
You get to rebuild the life of your dreams
So start with a strong foundation
From there the only way is up
Build a life with strength
Build a life full of your dreams
No one can take away

You deserve the life you are about to have
For you have shown you deserve it
You deserve the very best
That life has to offer
You have worked hard
You have worked hard for yourself
You have worked hard for those around you
You have worked hard for those in need
You deserve it all
You deserve all that life has to offer
Receive it as the blessing it is
Receive it for the blessing you are
For you deserve this and more

It doesn't matter what others think
It doesn't matter if they think you don't deserve it
They have no idea who you are inside
They have no idea what you have had to go through
They have no idea what it took for you to get here
They have no idea the battles you have faced
They have no idea the tears you have cried
The only thing that matters
Is you made it
You got there

Pay it forward
With love
Pay it forward
Without expectation
Pay it forward
To make a change
Pay it forward
In appreciation
Pay it forward
To change someones life
Pay it forward
To change someones world
Pay it forward
With love in your heart

You deserve everything you have ever dreamed of
Everything you have ever wanted
You deserve it
So believe in yourself
Believe in your dreams
Go out there and get them
For you deserve them
And so much more

I want you to shine
I want you to show you can do it
I want you to live your best life
I want you to show those who
thought you couldn't do it
Just how wrong they were
I want you to show them how amazing you are
But most of all
I want you to want this
I want you to do all this
FOR YOU

All the good things in life
Don't come easy
You have to take a risk
A risk for your happiness
A risk of the unknown
For anything worth having
Is worth the risk
Is worth your effort
Is worth your time

Sometimes when life doesn't go to plan
It works out better than what we had planned
So take a step back
Look at the situation
And appreciate what turn of events have happened
Look at how things have worked out better
How many more doors have opened
Because life didn't go to plan
So take it as a blessing
That your life didn't go to plan
It turned out better

Have the confidence in who you are
Have the confidence in what you are capable of
Have the confidence to pursue your passions
Have the confidence to be your authentic self
Have the confidence to go out and grab your dreams
And never let them go

Don't let your mind
Be your enemy
Don't let your mind
Talk you out of your dreams
Don't your mind
Be the reason you don't try
Don't let your mind
Be the reason for regrets
Don't let your mind
Be the reason you are not living your best life
Don't let your mind let you down

You are the creator of your reality
You can create anything you want
You can be anything you want
You can go anywhere you desire
You can create a home of your dreams
You can create the world around you
In any way you like
For you are the creator of your reality

Never regret anything in life
Never regret a day in your life
For you are here
For you have been given the blessing of life
Do you realise how many people
would give anything
Just to have someone they love
Be back in their life
Just to have one more day
To say I love you
To give them one more hug
Never regret a single moment in your life

You are destined for a life beyond your dreams
Keep believing in yourself
Keep believing in your dreams
Keep believing you deserve it
And greatness shall come
For you are destined for greatness
You are destined to shine

Everything you have wished for
Everything you have hoped for
Is going to work out
It is going to work out
Even better than you had imagined
For you have worked hard
You have not given up
You have kept going
Knowing that it will be all worth it
In the end
So keep going
Because it is going to work out

Live each day
As though each day
Has a happy ending
Then you shall live each day
Knowing it will end in happiness

Doing what's best for you
Is the hardest thing in the world
We spend our time
Our thoughts
Worried about what other people think
Worried about what other people will say
Worried about not disappointing people
More often than not
We put ourselves last
We need to start putting ourselves first
We need not to worry about other people
We need to start doing what's right
What's best for us

Live each day
As it was the first day of your life
Then you will live each day
As if it was the last day of your life

You are not who you once were
You are who you are now
As of this moment
You are you
Your best version
So do not live in the past
Do not let anyone else put you back in the past
Show them you have grown
Show them who you are now
Don't let them try to minimalise
how far you have come
You have worked to hard
If they can't except who you are now
Then you can't except them in your life

If you smile
You will feel happier
If you walk with pride
You will feel inner strength
If you walk with your head held high
You will feel pride
Everything you project on the outside
You will feel within
We are what we project out

The version of who you are now
Is strong
Stronger than you have ever been
Don't let anyone try and break you
For they will try to break you
For you have become someone they don't recognise
Someone who no longer puts up with their behavior
They don't like what they can no longer control
For you have shown how strong you are now
How you now know your worth
How you will no longer be available to anyone
Not worthy of your time or love
Stay strong and know your worth

It doesn't matter what it looks like
It doesn't matter how long it takes
It doesn't matter how far you have come
It doesn't matter where you have been
All that matters
Is where you are now
All that matters
Is where you are going

What has been lost to you
Was lost for a reason
For the universe saw what you couldn't see
It was removed to save you even more sadness
You have learned to disassociate from those
Who do not have your best interest at heart
Learn from this loss
Learn from these people
What you don't want
And what you will allow in your life
Look at that loss
As a blessing in disguise

Your imagination
Is your future
What you imagine
Is what is to come
For you have been given
The sight of imagination
To prepare for what is to come

Look for the magic in your life
Every day there is magic to be found
The sun came out
It warms your heart
The rain start
It fills your tank
The stars are shinning
They light the way
You got up today
Another day to be thankful for
You kissed your family
It melts your heart
There is so much magic in your life
Just start by looking for the little things
Then you'll see the big things

When a woman is hurt
She reevaluates her life
She believes in her self worth
She adjusts her crown
She picks up her sword
She becomes a warrior

You have come so far
Take the time to look back
And see just how far you have come
Don't be so hard on yourself
You have made miracles look easy
You have made life seem like walking
Through a sunfilled flower bed
Others see you and wonder how you do it
Others see you and are jealous of how
effortless you make it all seem
So don't be so hard on yourself
For you have come so far
You can go further than you think

Let the person you admire
Be the one who looks back at you
In the mirror

You were born to walk through life
With your heart bared
For all to heal
You were born to share
The love within your soul
For all to feel cherished
You were born to speak
From the heart
For all to feel loved
You were born to be shared
With the world
For the world needed you

Don't go chasing pretty things
Don't go chasing outside beauty
For beauty on the outside
Doesn't last
All you will have left
Will be an empty shell
An empty shell will collapse
And you will be left with nothing

Everyday we are learning
We never stop learning
No matter what our age
No matter what our education
There is always something to learn
Never think you have nothing to learn
Never think you don't need to learn
For then you will not grow
You will not evolve
Into the best you can be
Never stop learning

You are a shinning star
You were always
Meant to shine
You were always
Destined for greatness
You were always
Destined to be seen
So shine bright
Like you were always meant to do

You inspire the ones around you
You change those who have the
privilege to know you
For you see the world through eyes of love
You see that there is always a silver lining
You see that the world is truly a beautiful place
You see what a privilege it is to
be apart of this world
You know that everyday there is an opportunity
To change someones life
Everyday there is an opportunity
To change the world
You inspire all those
Who have the privilege to meet you
You are truly an inspiration
A gift to the world

Nothing stays the same
Every day is different
So the things you are worried about today
Will not be the same tomorrow
So don't waste your time today
On the same things that tomorrow
Will seem insignificant
Enjoy the here and now

You speak
People listen
For your words have meaning
Your voice was meant to be heard
Your words are spoken from the heart
Your words are spoken with kindness
Your words entice thought
Your words give peace
Your words heal the heart
Your words heal the soul
You were meant to speak
You were meant to be heard

Be kind to yourself
You have been through enough
Appreciate what you have been through
Appreciate how far you have come
So be kind to yourself
For you are worth that kindness
And so much more

You were meant to follow your dreams
If you follow your dreams
You will not be disappointed
You will not fail
For your dreams are there for you
To live the life you have imagined
To live a life
Of happiness
Of joy
Only you can make those dreams come true
Only you can take that first step
To make them happen
Only you can live a life
Of your dreams coming true
For they are your dreams
No one else's

Don't work so hard
Don't let life get in the way
Of having fun
For a life with no fun
Is a life of sadness

You have come so far
You have worked so hard
To get where you are
So don't give up now
Don't give up on you
You are worth every effort
You are worth every step
Every road, still to take
To get where you are going
In your life
You have come to far
To give up now

When life gets to much
Don't give up
Don't give up on you
Don't give up on your dreams
It's not an option
It's a choice to never give up

Don't let fear hold you back
Don't be afraid of what's to come
Don't be afraid of the unknown
Don't be afraid to succeed
For fear is only holding you back
From where you are meant to be
From where you are meant to shine
Success is only something to be fearful of
If you let it
If you allow it to change you
Keep being true to yourself
Keep being true to what's in your heart
Don't be afraid to shine

If you are dreaming about an amazing life
Don't just dream about it
Take action
Make those dreams come true
It is about creating a life you want
It's about you
Believing in yourself
Believing in your ability
To create that life you want

Life is filled with ups and downs
What matters is how you get back up
What you think about your time down
Do you get back up with vengeance
Or do you get back up
Appreciating your experience
Appreciate the struggle to get back up
How you forgive those who let you fall
How you forgive those who turned their back
When you were down
What matters is how you appreciate the ups
How you treat those on the way up
How you let go of the past
How you appreciate where you are now
How you look and help others still down
What matters in life is your choices
You choose to learn from the past
You choose to appreciate where you are now
You choose to appreciate life
It's up to you

When life gets hard
When things feel like there falling apart
Remember how strong you are
Remember how much you have already achieved
Remember how far you have come
You can get through this
You can do it, and come out the other side
Stronger than ever
You've got this
I have faith in you

You are stronger than you think
You are stronger than you feel
You are stronger now than ever before
Don't give up now
Don't let doubt beat you
Fight back
Fight for the life you want
Fight for the life you deserve
Fight
You will win
You will win in life
But you have to fight
For what you want
You have to fight
For you

You are worth it
You are worth the fight
Pick up your sword
And fight hard for you
You need to fight for you
For you are the most valuable person
That you need to fight for
So pick up that sword
And fight

You need to take a step
You need to step out of your mind
Step out of your fear
Step out of your darkness
You need to take the first step out
For that step will lead to many more steps
Before you know it
You will be walking
Then running
Running out of your darkness
Into your world of light
Into the place you were always meant to be
The place you were meant to shine
But you need to take that first step
Be brave

Everything so far
Has been a stepping stone
To the life you deserve
A stepping stone
To your happiness
A stepping stone
To your dreams
A stepping stone
To your future

Life is like a dance
Dancing everyday
Some days romantic
You are waltzing
Some days are fun
You are dancing the jive
Some days are hectic
You are rock and rolling
But as long as you are dancing through life
You are going to enjoy every day of it
So just keep dancing

Choose life
Choose to be happy
Choose to be kind
Choose to give
Choose to love
Life is a choice
Choose wisely

Follow your dreams
Chase your dreams
It may feel your dreams are like rainbows
No way to get there
That there is no end in sight
There is
Keep going
Every rainbow lands somewhere
You just have to follow it
To find your dreams
To make them happen
To find that pot of gold

Victory is yours
If you want it
All you have to do is try
Go out there and give it your best shot
You can do it
You can win
At this thing we call life

You are stronger than you know
You have the strength to carry on
You have the strength for greatness
You have fought and made it this far
You have the strength to keep going
You are not going to stop trying
You are not going to stop believing in yourself
You are not going to stop now
For you are stronger than you know
You have the strength to make it to greatness
You have the strength to make it to the end
You have the strength to get through anything
You have the strength to achieve
More than you will ever know

You are the key to your success
You are the key to your happiness
You are the key to living your dreams
So use that key and open the doors
To your best life

The sweetest flowers
Grow from the
Harshest conditions
The sweetest flowers
Thrive when life gets tough
The sweetest flowers
Stand tall
For all to see
The sweetest flowers
Have bloomed unexpectedly
Be the sweetest flower
In your garden
Stand tall for all to see

Have the confidence to step into the unknown
Have the confidence to take that leap of faith
For those steps are what are going to
lead you to your highest self
Those steps are going to let your true life begin
Those steps are going to make
your dreams come true
So have the confidence to take the first step
Then the next step will come easy

Your journeys path is about to become illuminated
For you to follow
Glowing bright with every step you take
To the destiny that awaits you
Follow that path you are on
You have taken the right road ahead
It shines for you to achieve your destiny
For you were meant to follow the path of greatness
You were meant to shine in all you do
Take the steps along the glowing path
You will not be disappointed
You will be living your dreams

We talk about learning lessons
We talk about how every day
There is something new to learn
We talk about healing
We talk about healing to move forward
Life
Life is our lesson
Life is our healing journey

The years fly by
Where have the days gone
Where have the dreams gone
Where have the loves gone
The years fly by
Don't let life pass you by
Don't live in lost dreams
Don't live in regret
Live knowing you are making memories
Live knowing you are making
your dreams come true
Don't let the years fly by without
living every moment of them

Life gets hard
It's hard doing what we know we must
But take it
One day at a time
Even one minute at a time
If you have to
For you have to put you first
Baby steps
Turn into big steps
Turn into leaps

You've seen the dark
Now you can live in the light
You appreciate that shinning light
That was ever present in the dark tunnel
Your glimour of light
Your glimour of hope
That beckond you to walk toward
That glimour of light that once you started
You ran to
For you saw that there was a way out
There was life at the end beckoning you
A life for you to live like never before
Appreciating every day
Filled with dreams
Filled with light

It's never too late
It's never too late to start over
It's never too late to say sorry
It's never too late to take that first step
It's never too late to become the best version of you
It's never too late to start living your best life
It's never too late

You have walked through the storm
You didn't get wet in the rain
You didn't get hit with the hail
You didn't get struck by lightning
You have come out the other side unscathed
The tears stopped flowing
Their words stopped hurting you
Their lies didn't strike where
they had wanted them to
You now know
You can dance in the rain

Never be afraid to be yourself
For you are perfect just the way you are
You were made to shine
You were made to love
You were made to change the world
You were made just perfect
So shine bright
Let the world see
Just how perfect you are

You are being seen
You may not think anyone is noticing you
They are
They are noticing your strength
They are noticing your words
Your words are powerful
Your words give others strength
Your words are saving lives
Don't ever think you are not making a difference
For you are
More than you will ever know
Keep using your words
Keep giving strength to those
Who need it most
I'm proud of you
Keep being you

You shine bright
You shine your light
Like a beacon of light
Shinning from a light house
For everyone around you
To feel bright
To feel safe
To feel loved
Keep shinning bright
Keep shinning your light

Everything in life takes time
Don't try and rush through life
You will miss the best parts
It's the little things
That mean the most sometimes
If you rush you'll miss them
Take the time to enjoy every moment
Don't miss anything
Enjoy all that life has to offer
Take your time
Enjoy every little moment

Where there is light
You will also find darkness
It's what you take with you
To fight that darkness
That matters
Never be afraid to fight for you
For the light is always better
Than the dark
You were meant to live bright
Not live in the dark

Such beauty surrounds us
Just waiting for you to explore
From the bush
To the sea
From the north
To the south
The world is a utopia
Just waiting for you
Go out there everyday
And enjoy our beautiful world
Whether you walk down the road
Or whether you fly across the world
There is beauty to behold
Just take the time to enjoy it
The world is out there waiting for you

Be positive
For you know how hard you have worked
For you know you deserve everything that is coming
Be positive in knowing it is all going to pay off
Be positive that the life you have worked so hard for
Is coming for you because you worked for it
You deserve it

Is there something in your life
That you are dreaming of
That you are just waiting for the right moment
When is the right moment
What are you waiting for
That moment may never come
Why put limitations on the moment
Limitations on when you can make the dream
Come true
Don't wait any longer
Go out and make that dream come true
Today

Life

Life is shinning bright
Every day and every night
Shinning bright
For the whole world to see
Just for you and just for me
Make sure you let your life
Shine bright
For the whole world to see

You are the magician of your life
You can make miracles happen
Miracles happen everyday
Just being alive is a miracle
Having the ability to dream
Having the sight to enjoy your surrounds
Having the privilege of giving and being loved
You can make the magic in your life happen
You don't need a wand
You just need spirit
You just need vision

What are you waiting for
Your life has already begun
Your life waits for no one
The days rush by
The nights just fly
Don't let life pass you by

Life is all about determination
Have you got the determination to keep going
To not give up
When things get tough
Have you got the determination to not let anyone
Tell you, you can not do it
Have you got the determination to
make your dreams come true
Life is all about not giving up
About have that determination
Nothing is going to stop me
Attitude

It just takes one person to believe in you
For you to have the confidence to start
To start the next chapter in your life
to have the confidence to make the changes needed
Thank god for that one person
That person made all the difference
That person was you

You are the master of your life
You control your happiness
You control your joy
You control your destiny
No one else but you
For you are the only one
Who knows what your dreams are
You are the only one
Who knows what's in your heart
So listen to your heart
And follow your dreams

Failure is just an noun
Keep trying
Until you turn it into a success
Never give up

You are a survivor
You have been through so much
All your life
You have endured when others would of given up
You have kept going knowing
you were meant for more
Knowing you were here for a reason
You are here today because you have courage
You had the strength to keep going
You have the strength to survive
You are a survivor

Remember who you are
Don't lose sight of who you are
Don't lose sight of what it is you want
Don't lose sight of where you are going
Don't let the world bring you down
Don't let set backs make you feel deflated
You are good enough
You are worthy
You are amazing
Remember just who you are

I know it gets hard sometimes
Just get out of your head
To stop the thoughts
You need to do it
You need to stop worrying about tomorrow
For tomorrow, who knows what will happen
You can't worry about something
you have no idea about
You can't worry about the past
It's over, it's been and gone
You can't change it
So you can't worry about it
If you spend your time
Worrying about yesterday or tomorrow
You can't enjoy today
Today will just slip by

They say, "don't go chasing rainbows"
Why not
Someone needs to find that pot of gold
All rainbows land somewhere
If you don't go chasing rainbows
What are you chasing
What are you doing with your life
Go out and chase your rainbow
Chase your dreams

Be your own hero
Be the hero of your life
Heroes fight for everyday
Heroes fight for the underdog
Heroes fight for justice
Heroes fight for life
Heroes fight for love
You have fought a good fight
You have fought everyday
To be the person you are now
You have fought everyday
To conquer your fears
You have fought everyday
To be the best version of you
Keep being your own hero

You need to believe in you
Before anyone else can
For what you believe
You project
So make sure you are projecting
How amazing you are
How special you are
How you believe in you

She walks along the street smiling
Everyone who sees her smile
Can't help but smile back
They don't know why they are smiling
She is an energy they can't help but notice
She is a walking bright light
They can't help but want to be part of
Can't help but smile at
Be that energy
That everyone wants to be part of
Be that person that evokes happiness from others
Be that person smiling at life
That person everyone smiles back at

Follow your destiny
Our lives have all been mapped out
We all have a destiny to follow
Whether you follow yours
Or take another path
Sooner or later
You will find yourself
Following the path destined for you
For you can not change what is destined
For you

Don't let your doubts stand in
the way of your dreams
Don't let your fear
Don't let your procrastination
Don't let your laziness
Don't let your attitude
Don't let others
Don't let bullies
Don't let haters
Don't let one mistake
Ruin your dreams
There your dreams
No one else's
No one can tell you your dreams
No one can tell you your dreams are wrong
No one can tell you how to live your life
No one can stop you trying
No one can stand in your way
Only you can stand in your way
Only you can stop them
Only you can give up
Why would you
Why would you stop living
Dream big

When the days are dark
As the storm enters
Lift your sword
For you are a warrior
Never forget that
Fight through the dark
Never forget you are the storm
So lift that sword and fight

You know you are doing well
When others are talking about you
When others are hating on you
When others are not happy for you
When others are trying to put you down
When others are intimidated by you
You know you are achieving your goals in life
When this happens
Not everyone is happy to cheer you on
Not everyone will appreciate your success
Not everyone will try to elevate you
Not everyone is happy in their own life
Unfortunately not everyone has
the same values as you
You keep being you

If no one has told you today
Simply
I'm proud of you

You are like a butterfly
A caterpillar
Encased waiting to emerge
Into a beautiful butterfly
Just waiting to show the world
Your beauty
Just waiting to emerge
And spread your wings
Just waiting to fly
Just waiting for you
To take off

It's not happening to you
It's happening for you
You need to look at things
With a different perspective
Why is this happening
What can I learn from this
What can I gain from this
Am I not lucky it happened this way
Remember, it's happening for you
Life is all about the way you perceive things

Life gets hard
Your dreams feel so far away
You have to work for your dreams
You have to really make an effort to achieve them
But you know what's harder
Not even taking the chance
Not working hard for your dreams
Sitting back years down the road
And regretting not trying
Regretting not believing in yourself
Regretting not having the discipline
to work hard for them
Don't be the one with regrets
Be the one that tried
Be the person who loves life
With no regrets

What is lost
Can be found
Do not think it is lost forever
Nothing that is lost
Cannot be found
With perseverance
With hard work
With belief
Search for it
You will find your way

Every day is another day
To go out there
And win
Another day
To face your fears
Another day
To start living life
Another day
To believe in yourself
Another day
To just keep trying
Because one day
You will win

You are enough
Don't let anyone make you believe different
Their opinion of you
Is just that
Their opinion
Not your truth
You know better
You know you are enough
Period

Believe in your happy ever after
Why can't you have it
You deserve it
Go after it
It's yours
Waiting for you
Reach out
And grab hold of it
With both hands
Have your happily ever after
Be happy

The only limits
In your life
Are the limits
You put on yourself

You are magical
You can do anything
You are admired
People are in awe of you
They wonder how you do it
They wonder if you truly are magical
It's your attitude that is magical
It's your heart that is magical
It's your soul that is magical
It's your pure presence that is magical
It's your kindness that is magical
It's your beliefs that are magical
Keep being magical
Keep being you

You start life with what you have been dealt with
It's up to you how you play the game of life
You can complain about what you have been given
Or you can become the dealer
You can play to win
How do you want to continue your life
The complainer
The dealer
Or the winner
Think about it

Trust
Trust in you
You need to have trust in you
Trust in your decisions
Trust in your heart
Trust in your soul
Listen when your heart
Speaks to you
Listen to your soul
When it calls out to you
Trust in you
For there is no one better
To have trust in
Than you

You truly are amazing
You've had a hard life
Everything you've been through
Everything you've conquered
And you are still standing
You are still smiling
You are truly amazing

Who cares what others think
Who cares what others do
Their entitled to their opinion
It doesn't affect you
Their actions are their problem
To clean up
You just keep being the beautiful person
You are
You keep thinking good thoughts
You keep doing great things
For your thoughts and actions
Define who you are
Define your heart within
That's all that matters

You don't owe anybody anything
You don't need to prove yourself to anyone
You don't need to prove it to the world
The only person you owe
The only person you need to prove it to
IS YOU

Remember who you are
Don't let anyone make you question
Your strength
Your ability
Your heart
Remember just how amazing you are
No one can make you feel less than you are
No one has the right to even suggest you are less
For you are perfect just as you are
For you were made perfectly
Don't let anyone question
Who you are

I'm looking for a good investment
I know investing is the way to success
I know I have to work hard on my investments
I know research is the way to find the best
I don't have to look anymore
I found my investment
I found the best investment out there
That investment
Is me

What are you waiting for
Enjoy every little thing
Make your dreams come true
Life is too short
To just sit back and wait
Just what are you waiting for
Tomorrow
It may never come
Next week
Will you still be where you are now
Still waiting
Just watching life pass you by
Go out there and enjoy your life
Don't wait
Because time is not waiting for you

Life is about the battle
Not the war
People see you fighting the war
They don't see you fighting the battle
The battle within
Win the war
Win your battle

When God made you
He broke the mould
He looked at you
And new he had made perfection
There was absolutely nothing he would change
For you are perfect
That is why
There is only
One of you
Perfect
In every way

You can stay where you are
Live life where it feels safe
Or you can take a chance
A chance on life
A chance on you
A chance to make your dreams come true
A chance to live everyday as an adventure
Are you going to take a chance
On you

Every set back
Every time something goes wrong
Is an opportunity
To change your life
To change your world
Look at it as a opportunity
For something greater
For something better than you had imagined
Look at it as the opportunity you never knew
You wanted
Every negative
Has a positive
If you look at it the right way
If you look at it as a blessing
To change your world

Everyday is a new day
A new chance
To start again

Don't let that idea you had
Sit there and be just an idea
Make it happen
Make that idea
Into reality
Reality that changes
Your life
Don't look back
In the years to come
And regret not tuning that idea
Into the life changing idea
It could be

Take time to stop
And enjoy life
It's the little things
That mean so much
Don't be so busy
That you let life pass you by
And miss the little things
That are worth so much more
Than you can imagine

Don't let your dreams
Become overwhelming dreams
Just take your dreams
One day at a time
One piece of action
At a time
Once it starts
It will just keep going
Until it comes true
Don't over complicate
Your dreams
There your dreams
There is no time limit
Just start
One day at a time
You can do it
You can make them happen

Have faith
Have patience
The good things in life
Take time
The great things in life
Take patience

Are you choosing you
Are you choosing your dreams
Are you putting you first
Your hopes and dreams first
You need to choose you
You need to put you first
You need to make your dreams happen
You need to make those dreams
Come true
Put you first
Choose you

You are unstoppable
Nothing and no one
Can stop you now
You will go after your dreams
And achieve them
You will go after everything
You have ever wanted
And achieve them
For you are
Unstoppable

Make your dream a reality
Take your imagination
Make it a reality
No one can do it
But you
No one can start it
But you
No one can dream it
But you
No one can make it a reality
But you
You are the one
Who can make it happen
You are the one
Who needs to believe
In yourself
No one else
But you

You are glowing
You are glowing from within
Your glow is bursting from your soul
For the whole world to see
Just how beautiful you are
Now look in the mirror
And see
What everyone else sees
You are truly beautiful
You are glowing

No one said you can't change your mind
No one said you can't change your dreams
No one said you can't change your goals
You can do anything you want
You can change anything you want
It doesn't matter what anyone else thinks
It doesn't matter what anyone else says
The only one it affects is you
The only one you need to make happy is you
Change whatever you need
To make you happy
Change whatever you can
To get to where you are living
Your best life
Do it for you

The ability to sit on ones own
In silence
In patience
In reflection
Is the ability to know ones worth

What gets you up in the morning
What gets you smiling when you open your eyes
What gets you motivated in your day
I hope it's your future
I hope it's you making your dreams come true
I hope it's you living you best life
I hope it's you knowing you can do anything
You set your mind to
I hope you make yourself smile
Every day
Making those hopes and dreams
Come true

When you find
Your own happiness
Within
Then you can
Share it

Don't let anyone tell you
What matters
What you should feel
What your life should look like
Your life is but your own
Let no one tell you to be their clone
Your life matters to no one
But you alone
So be the one
You make proud
You be the one
Who dances on a cloud

Don't block what is coming for you
Don't put up barriers
Don't turn a blind eye
Don't stop believing
That you deserve everything
For you do deserve everything
Coming for you and more
Welcome it all in
With open arms
For you deserve it

Life feels hard
Life feels lonely
You feel like you just want to
Stay under the covers
I promise you
These feelings will pass
Get up
Pick yourself up
There is to much life to live
There are to many people
Just wishing they had your life
Just wishing they could meet
Someone like you
Just wishing you would notice them
Life is just waiting for you to get up
And start living again

Don't fear the unknown
Life is a series of unknowns
Every day we wake up to the unknown
We never know exactly what the day will bring
You take that chance everyday in getting up
You take the chance in your every day
None of us ever know what will happen in the day
So do not fear going after your dreams
Don't fear the unknown in life
Or life will pass you by

Make sure you are giving
Your time
To those who
Appreciate it
Your time
Is precious
No one knows
Just how much time
We have
So give your time
Only to those
Who will truly
Value it

Never think you are not enough
You are more than worthy
Of all you can imagine
Of all your dreams coming true
Of all the love that embraces you
You are perfect just the way you are
You are more than worthy of this
And so much more
Never think you are not enough

If you are looking for perfection
Don't come looking here
I'm not perfect
But I am perfectly
Broken
I put my broken pieces back
I pick them up
Each time they fall
And carefuly place them
Back where they belong
I have many cracks
To prove just how many times
I have been broken
But these are the cracks
That show I have picked myself up
And put me back together
For I am strong enough
To fix myself
I am perfectly broken

Pay attention to your challenges
Pay attention to missed opportunities
Don't mistake a challenge
As a negative
Pay attention
Turn it into a positive
Don't let that opportunity
Slip by

They say treat people right on the way up
For they will be the ones you are passing
On the way down
But why is there a top
Or a bottom
Why can't there just be
Today everything is going right
Today is working out as planned
Today I am proud of myself
Today you give encouragement
To your friend
To your neighbour
To a stranger
Today is a good day to be a good person

Kindness comes from the soul
Your light comes from the heart
Your words come from the mind
No one can change
What's buried within

Succeed on your own
You do not need anyone else
To endorse your success
You do not need anyone else
To approve your success
You do not need anyone else
To say, well done, you did it
Your own validation
Is enough
You knew you could
And you did

You are never to old
To start again
Every day is your new start
Take the first step
To start again
You can do it

She believed in herself
When others didn't
She believed in her heart
When others broke it
She believed in her soul
When others let go
She believed in her mind
When others let her down
She believed in her own self worth
When others thought they could do better
She believed she could
And so she did

If you keep living in the past
How are you going to live in the now
How are you going to live in the tomorrows

You love the people around you
Being happy
You love to see them shine
You love to know you may of been
Just some small part in that
But in order to enjoy their happiness
You have to be happy in yourself
You have to make sure you shine
You have to believe in your own worth
In order to be truly happy
For everyone else

Put you first
You are the most important person
In your life
Once you are your priority
Then you can start to give to others
Then you can prioritise others in your life
Then you can show others just what you are made of
Then you can give to them from the heart with love

No one can make you feel unworthy
No one can make you feel unloved
No one can make you feel worthless
No one can make you feel not enough
Unless you let them
For you know you are everything
They say you are not
That's what scares them
That's what makes them jealous
That's what makes them less than you
That's what makes you a better person
Than they will ever be

It takes strength
To stand up for what
You believe is right
What you believe is unfair
What you believe should be said
What you believe what should be done
Have strength to stand up
For what is right

Feel proud of who you are
Feel proud of how far you have come
Feel proud of all you have achieved
Feel proud of just being you
Don't let anyone make you feel less than you are
Don't let anyone make you feel bad
for what you have over come
Don't let anyone make you feel bad
for what you have achieved
You don't need anyone to be proud of you
Feel proud of you everyday

You need to just see what people really think
Just what they are really saying about you
Just what their intentions really are
Just what their plans are for your future together
Before you fall hard into your ideas
About who they really are

Be with someone
Who makes you feel
Nothing less than
Amazing
Special
Beautiful
Loved
The only person on earth
Every day
Expect nothing less
You deserve it
Know your worth

Karma is real
She is always watching
She is always waiting
For the exact time
To cause the most impact
Be kind always
For karma is watching

Our homes are safe
They are our safe haven
When things get tough
We just want to go home
We just want to stay home
Where we feel safe
Don't take the luxury
Of having a home
The luxury of your home
For granted
Having a home
Is a blessing

What you allowed in your life
What you put up with yesterday
Is not what you will allow today
Not what you will put up with tomorrow
For who you once were
Is not who you now are
Or who you will be tomorrow

Embrace you
Embrace every part of you
Your strength
Your wisdom
Your heart
The warrior with in
Embrace it all
For that is what makes you
Who you are
What makes you so special
What makes the powerful
Person you are
The person who has gone through
So much
And come out the other side
Stronger
You are a fighter
Embrace you
For you are special

If people don't realise
Just how amazing you are
Just how special you are
Just what you bring to the world
If they can't see your worth
They are not worth your time
They are not worth even one second
Of your thoughts
They are not worthy of you

I am so very proud of you
You have come so far
I know you have such a long way to go
I know every day is a struggle
A battle with yourself
But look how far you have come
I am so very proud of you
Keep going
Never give up
You are the one who is going
To make it
You are the one who will achieve it
You are the one who gives others hope
Hope that is they try hard enough
They to will do it
Never give up on your dreams
Never give up on you

You may not understand what I do
You may not understand what I say
You may not understand my ways
You may not understand me
But that's ok
For I know
You don't need to

The most beautiful rainbows
Come after the harshest storm
Life is like rainbows and storms
You shine bright
You smile
You are living life
But I know you shed many tears
I know some days it was hard to find your smile
But what you are doing now
Is living your life
Live your best life
Full of rainbows
Full of colour
Yes it will storm again
But you know that rainbow is coming
Everytime
Storms are hard but make you shine and sparkle
Even brighter afterwards
Never lose your sparkle

Just remember
Every new day
Is the first day
Of the rest of your life

You are strong

You are powerful

You are beautiful

You are special

You are amazing

You are a warrior

Live your life

Remembering this

Each and every day

Never forget

Just how blessed you are

Every tear you cry
Karma is collecting them all
Karma is counting each one
She knows where they come from
She knows just when to strike
The person who made you cry
Karma is keeping score

I'm right here
On the side lines
Cheering you on
Because I know you can do this
I know you can beat this
I know you can win
I'm so proud of you
I'll be here for you
Every step of the way
Here to give you strength
Whenever you need it
Whenever you are feeling low
Remember you are doing this for you
Because you deserve it
You are worth it
You deserve to be the very best you can be
You deserve to live your best life

Our past has made us
Who we are today
Our future will be
Who we decide we will be
It's up to you
Who do you
Want to be

When you're feeling weak
When you're feeling low
When you're feeling like
You want to give up
I want you to go
Look in the mirror
See why you started this
See the man who deserves your strength
See the man who can win this
See the man who deserves you to keep going
Don't give up
You are worth the fight
Keep going

You hold the key
To your happiness
You are the key
To your happiness
Don't be afraid to unlock
The next door
The next door to the rest
Of your life

Walk away from what no longer serves you
To make room for the happiness
You deserve
You worked to hard in life
To sit back and just let it pass you by
To have a life with no happiness
You deserve the best in life
You deserve that happiness
So walk away from what no longer serves you
And find your happiness
You deserve it

You are strong
Look how far you've come
Look what you have endured
You put your amour on
And the warrior appears
To win the war on life
Never forget the warrior within
Never forget just how strong you are

You thought you could break her
Break her spirit
Break her
Break her down
Down to your level
You didn't break her
You don't have that much power
What you did in fact do
Is make her stronger
She rose like the phoenix she is
She showed you just how strong she is
You couldn't break her
She will never give you that much power
That's her power within
She will never give that power away
For she knows her worth
She knows her strength
She knows who she is
She is a warrior

I know it will be hard
I know it will be a battle
The battle may have started
The battle within
I want you to now
Win the war

You have had to endure
More than anyone should
You have had to fight the demon
You once loved
But you are strong
You are brave
You can do this
You can win
Because you are worthy
Because you are loved
Because you deserve to win

Live your life
Like everyday
Is your last
Love your life
Like everyday
Is magical
Live your best
Life

She dreamed it
She didn't believe them
When they said she couldn't have it
She didn't believe them
When they said she couldn't do it
She didn't believe them
When they said she will never make it
She didn't believe them
When they said she wasn't worthy
She didn't believe them
So she went out there
And showed them
Just what she was made off
Showed them she could have it all
Showed them she could do anything
Showed them just how wrong they were
She went out there
And she showed them

Pick up your sword
For today is a new day
To go out there and fight
Fight for you
Fight for the life you want
Fight for everything you have dreamed of
For you are the only one who can fight for it
You are the only one who can pick up your sword
And go out there and slay each and every day
For you

She was let down again
Her light was dimmed a little more
Her head hung a little lower
Her shoulders hunch a little rounder
She took a moment of self pity
Then she realised just who she is
Just how worthy she is
Remembered her strength
Remembered no one could make her feel this way
If she didn't let them
So she stood a little taller
She straightened her shoulders
She put her head back
And walked with pride
Knowing that once again
She would rise above it all
Rise like a phoenix
Show the world
She's got this

If it doesn't bring you joy
If it doesn't serve you
If it doesn't make you smile
If it doesn't make you want to
Get up and start the day with gusto
You need to walk away
You need to find your joy

Maybe I'm not meant to find love
Maybe I'm not meant to be a half
Maybe I'm not meant to hold a hand
Maybe I'm meant to hold many hands
Maybe I'm meant to heal other hearts
Maybe I'm meant to be others strength
On their journey
Maybe I'm meant to be a voice for the
Voiceless
Maybe this has been the plans
For me all along
Maybe I should keep being me

Walk away in peace
Leave behind the war
Don't look back

We walk every day
Not really knowing
Where we will end up
At the end of the day
But we have faith
That we will be
Where we are meant
To be
Keep the faith
In every day
Knowing you will end up
Where you are meant to be

You are worth finding
Everything you can imagine
You are worth achieving
Everything
You can dream of
You are worthy
Never forget
You are worthy
Just because you are you

Today
Is the first day
Of the rest of your life
So start with all the changes
You have wanted to make
Start with all the dreams
You never thought you could have
For today is the day
To start it all
For today
Is the first day
Of the rest of your life

Why do we look for the unattainable
Why do we think we can have it
When all along they have no intention
Of ever obtaining us
Because we know we deserve the unattainable
We know we are worthy of great things
We know one day when the time is right
We will indeed obtain
The unattainable

I see you there
Sitting alone
I wonder what you are thinking
I wonder what you are planning
I wonder if you think you are enough
I see you looking
I wonder who you are looking for
What you are looking for
I wonder if you found
What you are looking for
I hope you look within
For everything you are looking for
Is already yours
For you are everything you need
You are already everything you could want
Just look within

One day
Someone will look at you
Like their life will not be worth living
If you are not in it

Find your joy
Find your happiness
Find the love within
Find the person you always knew you were
Let that person shine for all the world to see
Don't hide that beautiful person away
The world needs you
It needs that beautiful person within
It needs your happiness and joy spread around
Take the time to shine and shine
bright for everyone to see

Tell me
Do you really think
You deserve it
Really feel you deserve it all
Because you do
You deserve it all
And so much more
Never forget
You deserve it all

Have patience
It is all just waiting for you
Your future is already planned out for you
Maybe you have deviated of the path
Maybe you need to find the path
Of your true journey again
Just have patience
In the knowing
It will all work out for you
All your dreams will come true
What was meant for you
Will not pass you by
Have faith

Sitting alone
Just watching the waves roll in
Listening to roar of the ocean
Is the best place to be
To find you
What you really want
What you really need
To find the peace within

You don't need anyone else
To be happy
Find the happiness within
For true happiness is found
Within our selves
When you find that happiness
You will attract the right person
That is meant for you
That person that will make you
Feel like you have never felt before
Like you have been blessed
From above
But you need to find it within
Before you can find it on the outside

Take the time to heal
Take the time to grow
Take the time to be you
Take the time to find you
Take the time and don't feel guilty

How lucky are we
To be alive
Just to wake up every morning
To be able to walk outside
And enjoy the air we breathe
The peace we live in
Because so many don't have it
Appreciate just being you
Just having the life you have
So many dream of the life
You have

I hope you are ready
Ready for all your blessings
That are coming for you
For you deserve everything
That has been waiting for you
It's all there just waiting
I hope you are ready
For the beauty that is coming

Everything happens for a reason
So everything that is happening now
Is happening for a reason
Even though you can't see it
Doesn't mean it's not happening
So take a step back
And appreciated everything
That is happening now
In knowing it won't be forever
Knowing it is for a reason
And that reason
Is you

They may think they got away with it
They may think they have won
But what they don't know
Is, it wasn't a game to you
You have more integrity than that
They also have not got away with anything
For eventually they will have karma
For everything they have done

You have them in wonderment
For they thought they had broken you
They thought they would bring you down
They thought they would of destroyed your essence
They thought they could turn the world against you
With their lies and accusations
What they didn't know was it
only made you stronger
It only made you more determined
not to be like them
It only gave you more energy to
achieved everything you wanted
Now they sit back and see that you
are living your best life
And they are wondering how you are doing it
With everything they threw at you
They didn't expect you to rise like a phoenix
And show the world who you really are
But in doing so
Show the world who they really are

Don't be fooled by the outside
True beauty is within the heart
The outside beauty can be a lie
Only the inside beauty
What's in the heart
Is what's real
The only beauty
You should love

The only person you can control
Is you
You can not control anyone else
Nor should you want to control them
If you are wanting to changed them
Wanting to control them
Look in the mirror
Look at the relationship
For the right person
The right relationship
Is not one you find fault in
Not one you want to change
The right one
Is perfect
Just the way they are

Your silence
Is more powerful
Than you realise

You are brave
You are strong
You are all you need
For your new beginning
For your new life
For the new you
Start now
Get your courage out
And make the change
You have been
Dreaming of

You can't tell a lier
The truth
They already
Believe
Their own lies

Life has given you roses
It's in the way
You hold them
That makes all the difference
Hold them wisely
Watch how beautiful they bloom
Hold them with disregard
Feel how you will be stung
When life gives you roses
Hold them wisely

Your dreams
Start with a thought
Every thought is a dream
Every dream is your reality
Just waiting for you to believe
Just waiting for you to make
Come true

The storm you endured
Was harsh
The storm you made it through
Was dark
The storm you came out shinning
Was a storm you thought you'd never
Have to walk through
Never have to battle
But you did
You made it
You may of come out wet
But you came out clean
Be proud of how you endured

If you live your life
In truth
In love
In forgiveness
With good intentions
You will never
Regret a day
In your life

Appreciate every minute
Appreciate every moment
Appreciate the time you have
Appreciate the life you live
Appreciate the people you love
It sounds simple
But how often do you think
I wish
If only
If only is now
I wish is now
Make sure you appreciate
Every day
And
Everyone

When you are at your worst
You see people at their best
You see people for who
They really are
Some step up
Some surprise you
Some melt away
Some are your biggest
Disappointment

Your attitude
Is everything in this life
You can choose to be mean
You can choose to be jealous
You can choose to be nasty
You can choose to be kind
You can choose to be caring
You can choose to be forgiving
You can choose to be loving
It is up to you
What do you choose
Your attitude
Is everything in this life

I'm proud of me
I'm proud for overcoming
Everything that has been thrown at me
I'm proud for not coming down to your level
I'm proud for standing up for what is right
I'm proud of not holding back and trying my best
I'm proud of the fight I have in me
To be the very best I can be

Don't accept others behaviour
Of you or your life
It's your life
Not theirs
You be assured in your life
You be assured in your behaviour
Let their behaviour show who they are
Let them live their life
Away from yours
You stand tall
In your life

We can not always choose
What falls onto our life's path
But we can choose
How and when
Or even if
We pick it up

You could argue your point
You could tell your story
You could share your life
But would they listen
Listen like they do
When you are silent
For your silence
Speaks louder than you could imagine
Your silence
Speaks volumes

If you knew me
You don't know me
For I am not who I was
I am who I am now

We always worry
About what others think
About what others are saying
About what others are feeling
But the only one who you should be worried about
Is you
What you think
What you say
What you are feeling
Worry about you

The louder you are
The more they can't hear you
Be quiet
In everything you do
Be quiet in everything you say

Watch how you are now heard
We all have skeletons
We all have a past
Be proud of your past
Be proud of who you are today
For your past has made the person you are
Be proud of how far you've come
Be proud of all you have achieved
Be proud of the person you are becoming
Just be proud of you
Everyday

Milton Keynes UK
Ingram Content Group UK Ltd.
UKHW040254181024
449757UK00001B/13

9 781964 744612

Excerpt from Code Wolf

"Are you fuckin' with me?"

"No, Randall, I assure you I am not fuckin' with you," Rafe Maccon eased his immense frame back into his oversized, black leather chair and narrowed his ice blue eyes at his Third and one of his oldest friends. How long had he known the man sitting in front of him?

Randall had come to Maccon City when Rafe was about ten, he looked the same then as he did now. Tall at six foot three inches, muscular, and more than a little intimidating to the Wolves under him with his long beard and equally long dark brown hair.

Rafe, however, was the Alpha. He was more amused than intimidated by his surly friend.

EXCERPT FROM CODE WOLF

"A vacation?! What the fuck am I gonna do on a vacation? Come on, Rafe, this is bullshit!"

The door to Rafe's private office flew open and in strolled a very happy, very pregnant Charley Maccon, Rafe's wife. The Alpha's eyes glowed as they landed on his positively glowing mate. She wore a long, flowy dress. The shade was a pale-yellow color that, Randall admitted to himself, looked damn good with her creamy complexion and curly dark hair.

Their Alpha Female was quite something. There wasn't a Wolf Guard in the place who wouldn't lay down his/her life for her.

"Well, maybe you should consider a vacation to be a relaxing experience, Randy," she dropped a kiss on Randall's cheek and walked past him, over to her husband whom she kissed full on the mouth.

The way his Alpha's eyes homed in on her when she opened the door was nothing compared to the hungry gaze that followed her across the room.

Randall had noticed it took a while for Rafe to get used to his mate's habit of greeting everyone with a kiss or hug. Wolves were protective of their mates, but Randall thought his Alpha was doing an exceedingly good job of hiding his tension. Werewolves did not share very well.

Charley; however, had stood firm. That was the

way she was raised, and she wasn't going to change for any, how had she put it? Neanderthal browbeating husband, regardless of how cute his ass was!

Randall had no direct knowledge if the "cute ass" statement was true or not. And he didn't want to know. He liked Charley though, had from the beginning. He was musically inclined and often took to one of the common rooms to strum his guitar or play a few keys on the piano.

About the Author

C.D. Gorri is a USA Today Bestselling author of steamy paranormal romance and urban fantasy. She is the creator of the Grazi Kelly Universe.

Join her mailing list here: https://www.cdgorri.com/newsletter

An avid reader with a profound love for books and literature, when she is not writing or taking care of her family, she can usually be found with a book or tablet in hand. C.D. lives in her home state of New Jersey where many of her characters or stories are based. Her tales are fast paced yet detailed with satisfying conclusions.

If you enjoy powerful heroines and loyal heroes who face relatable problems in supernatural settings, journey into the Grazi Kelly Universe today. You will find sassy, curvy heroines and sexy, love-driven heroes who find their HEAs between the pages. Werewolves, Bears, Dragons, Tigers, Witches, Romani, Lynxes, Foxes, Thunderbirds, Vampires, and many more Shifters and supernatural creatures dwell within her worlds. The most important thing is every mate in this universe is fated, loyal, and true lovers always get their happily ever afters.

Want to know how it all began? Enter the Grazi Kelly Universe with Wolf Moon: A Grazi Kelly Novel or pick up Charley's Christmas Wolf and dive into the Macconwood Pack Novel Series today.

For a complete list of C.D. Gorri's books visit her website here:

https://www.cdgorri.com/complete-book-list/

Thank you and happy reading!

del mare alla stella,
   C.D. Gorri

Follow C.D. Gorri here:
   http://www.cdgorri.com

https://www.facebook.com/Cdgorribooks
https://www.bookbub.com/authors/c-d-gorri
https://twitter.com/cgor22
https://instagram.com/cdgorri/
https://www.goodreads.com/cdgorri
https://www.tiktok.com/@cdgorriauthor

Printed in Great Britain
by Amazon